manifests

Brendan McEntee

illustrations by Don Zirilli

ISBN: 10 0692193987
ISBN-13: 978-0692193983

for Virginia

manifests

ACKNOWLEDGMENTS

My deepest gratitude & thanks to Don Zirilli
for his patient readings, insights, illustrations
and care which helped make this book possible.

Found Photos

Photos of us, found
in an album I didn't
know you'd assembled—
where no trouble lived and lives
on. Memory, like
music, decays: the mind has
no history, allows your

laugh, your smiles, your tears
and indignations to thrive
and color the gray,
gives relief to the darkness
and the silences I serve.

In Water, In Air

No one's at the dock
when I kneel and pour a vial
of you in the lake —
current-carried through milfoil.
Then east, up the fire
road, park, walk the western wind,
pushing hard against the sun.

No one's on the crest
when I kneel and pour a vial
of you in the air —
current-carried through the sky,
there, and gone in the last light.

In the Atlantic

We've left land behind.
Treading, air raggedly pulls,
guts my mouth: heart, lungs
burn. I think about stopping,
about sinking beneath.
I let your ashes
fall into sinuous waves,

see you carried out
and under, churning, weaving
into the ocean you always
loved. Returning to the shore
—I am left behind, drowning.

Spun Out So Far

Back in '08, right
before everything broke down —
years I can't clearly
remember — when we would dance
as we pleased: on rocks,
in snow, in the rainy dark,
unseen in the known,
nameless, in the blind love-lights
where angels hover.

Endurance as grace:
all is known — displeased, dispersed
in dark and in light.
Nothing known — spiritual
spoilage stopped: blindness remains.

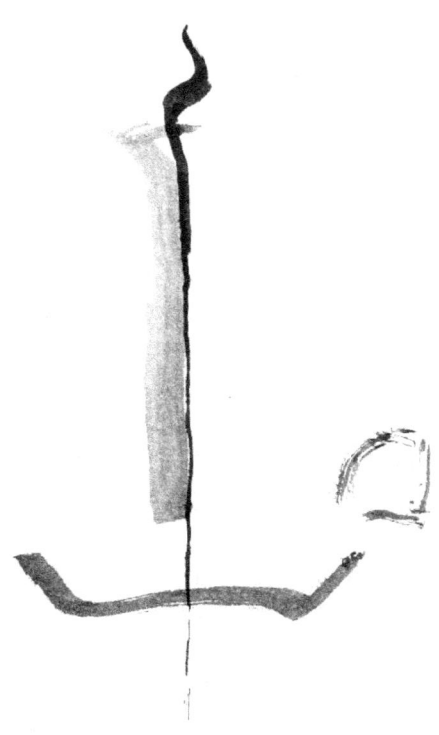

Have Memories

This Havisham-fear:
preserved life falls to decay.
Time, like rats, eats thought.
The Journey becomes Vigil;
objects to relics —
books, clothing and paints: unspoiled
scents — some holy hostages

in a Memory
Palace, stories rotting out
behind groomed hedge-knots.
I, guttered altar candle,
archaic and dumb, attend.

Up Against

Take my name and fade
against the fire, unable
— unwilling? — to turn
around. Scars reflect absence,
that negative space
of living which gets filled with
transcendent words and objects

of hope: fingernails
clawing in sand. There's
pleasure in misery; joy
in abnegation. Skin, bones
and breath live, invisible.

Light the Shadows

Sand brushed from your feet;
you show your skewed, highway smile.
We're self-imagined
human kintsugi, fixing
each other to new,
reforming and re-seaming,
replacing hurt history.

Removing your light
removes all shadows, creates
a different truth-lamp.
I fumble for golden seams
searching those roads, searching you.

Angle

An arc, not a bow:
refraction and diffusion.
"Somewhere" is your home:
from fire to water, earth, air,
newly adapted. Unfixed
to place and now, time—
I get to find you again

just beyond the reach
where a rainbow touches down
racing to harvest
your singular aspect from
the dread spiritus mundi.

The Purpose of a Commute

In dusk, my headlights
cast our house in stark relief
in the purpled air.
Music pushes through the
sheer curtain, billowing,
dispersing in the last sun,
becoming air that I hold

anticipating.
Our dog whines — you wait
until she settles,
open your arms for me: I
settle into your embrace.

Floating In Space

We take driving turns
across stone curves and aspects
that let us embrace
our transience. Beech,
hardwoods and softwoods—hemlock
maple, yellow birch,
fir—shear up through slate mountains,

through barns, from sideways—
this: the sacred secular.
I drive and you sleep;
you drive and I stare out,
our fingers remaining twined.

Brendan McEntee

Blind Anticipation

Cascading water;
we stop on our walk, watch
birds flit in the spray. You
always hold your breath,
smiling, anticipating
something I don't ever see.
My blindness always makes you

laugh. Single bird calls
rise above the rush. We walk on,
you with your cane,
slowly, me behind, watching
anticipating, you, us.

"It Would Be Nice to Think So"

Chimney smoke bends, folds
into wind-thrown rain beyond
the glass. My mordant
defect snuffles and wakes up.
With your favorite
mug—lightly chipped, lightly crazed
—your legs and feet tucked under,

you watch me watch rain
until you rise and curl in
against me, your kiss
serving as a reminder,
a prayer to salve and to save.

Piccata

An orchestral pass,
an exhalation, a tilt
of your chin, pouring
stock onto the pan, stepping
away from the steam.
Contented in your kitchen,
you toast the meal with your wine.

Ice-rime on the wood
melts onto the slate. I prop
my boots near enough
to dry out, take the proffered
spoon, tell you that it's perfect.

First Frost

An early killing
frost—I remove impromptu
shrouds of sheets, blankets
and our towels covering
your gardens, survey
what may be saved, see the toll
the night took in withering.

You spend the day bent,
trenching, cutting, rooting out,
planning the next year's
plantings, while decaying notes
of wind-chimes pass over you.

The Moment You Gave Up

You put down your brush,
your terra cotta pots half
painted with flowers,
sigh, snap your lighter: the last
time you'll touch them.
Three years later: clean brushes
and dried paint jars are reviewed,

closed up and returned.
The comfort of their presence,
even unseen, cedes
found mercy to new sorrow:
objects provide fresh access.

Induced Ingress

One a.m. arrives —
you climb under our flannels;
I roll toward you,
my warm hand on your warm side
settling into sleep.
I kiss the back of your neck,
drift off in you: skin; scent, breath.

Three a.m. arrives
I roll toward your blank space —
wake and remember,
look across the room's darkness
to your photo and your urn.

Down the Waterfall

...and as the flames unfurl,
enveloping sound and self....
You walked into dust-
night with a conspiracy
of silent ravens.
Elsewhere, waters roar, foam, spray:
and I, buffeted, look down

on broken boulders
and jagged tree limbs, shaking
in the pounding falls.
It's a one-way street, these falls: does
your desert live below?

Brendan McEntee

Your Dark

After the Great Fight
you call, all terror and tears
and I —I return,
back to your panic, hold you
in your rigid dread:
guttural, wild-eyed, undone.
You slept—I watched the night grow,

then fade, debating
myself as you restored your
poise and silenced all
future talk with a simple
"I'm sorry." I saw you lost
and right then, I was all in.

Breathless Charm

I push aside chairs,
coffee table, clear the space
turn up the music
— Sinatra, this time around —
and waltz, swing, foxtrot
and hold you, moving around
our living room. Sometimes, we

sway. I lead, you look
beautiful, life-flushed, beloved
and in love. The music ends
and we're still dancing,
for this lifetime or so more.

Meet Cute

I waited, squinting
into the gloom of your store,
watched you count out change
before unlocking
your door and letting me in.
My breath of recognition
quickly stifled by duty.

You — singular grace,
a sharp-eyed, smiling beauty —
not yet hollowed out
by time or loss or our life,
unlocked our door, let me through.

Background Fading

Flowers were never
an appropriate token.
Excepting the cuts
from your garden, you preferred
them live. I tended
to the dead, aging in stale
water, rendered to compost.

In final photos,
you work through roots, seeds
and soil. But weeds are patient,
like sand, like rocks, taking theirs
back, a violent erasure.

Ashes in Your Garden

I hand-dig these holes,
the shovel unusable—
hitting and chipping
stone—my fingers are faster.
First in your "chuckle
patch," the careless, air-thrown seeds
that flourished under your hand.

Then in your lilacs,
cultivated and then groomed:
under the hued fronds—
aubergine and baby blue—
arresting; where you now rest.

Lot's Wife

I haunt memories,
playing a pathologist
to photos and past:
the places of your first kiss;
your dog's death; your dad's
disgrace; places where you lost
love and innocence,
found damnation in spirits,
found a home in a dreamer

who could only fail
to lift you, save you from you
and your endless need
to look back at presumed ruins
of a fruitlessly lived life.

Troy

This is where we start....
You, naked before the fire,
your small self ablaze.
Heat pulses, birch skin curls, flares;
satisfied, giddy,
you leap, laughing, back to bed,
all avidity.

The cabin thrums, glows:
orange and yellows tumble,
pitch Phoenix shadows
on you. Of course: after all,
what else could you ever be?

ABOUT THE AUTHOR

BRENDAN MCENTEE studied literature at Hofstra University, where he acquired his Masters in English Literature. He is the author of the poetry collection, *Servicing Nostalgia.*

ABOUT THE ILLUSTRATOR

DONALD ZIRILLI is a sometimes poet, photographer, and artist. He was the editor of *Now Culture* & the art editor of the *Shit Creek Review* and the author of the poetry collection *Heaven's Not for You.*

www.ingramcontent.com/pod-product-compliance
Lightning Source LLC
Chambersburg PA
CBHW070354130626
46556CB00007B/3167